WHO Designs Roller-Coasters?

Dear Reader

Roller-coasters are exciting to look at and to ride. I've always wondered how they are made and who makes them. Finding out how they work and getting the answers to my other questions was exciting, too!

DID YOU KNOW ... IT TAKES ALMOST TWO YEARS TO PLAN AND BUILD A NEW ROLLER-COASTER.

Chris Gray works for a company in the USA that designs and builds roller-coasters. He loves his job!

During my interview with Chris Gray, I was amazed by how much work was involved in building roller-coasters.

I hope you enjoy reading about roller-coasters as much as I loved learning and writing about them!

Sharon Parsons

My sincere thanks to the following people for their time, information, images and enthusiasm for this book:

Chris Gray and his team at Great Coasters International, Sunbury, Pennsylvania, USA.

NELSON
CENGAGE Learning™
For learning solutions, visit cengage.com.au

Contents

WHO Designs Roller-Coasters?

1 A Roller-Coaster Designer

A **Love** of Roller-Coasters

Chris Gray

When Chris Gray was eight years old he was fascinated by roller-coasters. He wondered how they worked and how they stayed on the tracks.

From the age of eight, he collected pictures and information about roller-coasters.

> IT'S HARDER TO GET A JOB AS A ROLLER-COASTER ENGINEER THAN AS A HOLLYWOOD SUPERSTAR!
>
> CHRIS GRAY

A Dream Job Awaits

Chris's dream job was to work as a roller-coaster engineer. But his parents wanted him to get a different job. Chris never forgot his love for roller-coasters.

In later years, he went to a school to study subjects that would help him work in roller-coaster design.

THE LISEBERG Roller-COASTER

SWEDEN

For years, Chris carried a picture of his favourite roller-coaster – the Liseberg – in his wallet.

Did Chris ever go to Sweden to ride the Liseberg roller-coaster?

the Liseberg roller-coaster

LOOK AT PAGE 20

Roller-Coaster Models

After Chris finished school he started his own business. For four years, Chris made wooden models of amusement rides and roller-coasters for other companies.

Most of all, Chris enjoyed making models for a company called Great Coasters.

Chris with a model in his new business

A Great Logo

Most companies have a logo. Look at this logo and you can quickly see what the company does because it includes a roller-coaster. That's a great logo! A logo may use drawings, photographs, fonts, different colours, and shapes in its design. It identifies or "brands" the organisation or company, or person.

A Dream Comes True

Four years later, Great Coasters employed Chris as an engineer.

the Kentucky Rumbler

Today Chris has a new job at Great Coasters. He is the Director of Procurement and Assembly. He designs roller-coasters and checks if they are built correctly and are safe to use.

Chris often travels to roller-coaster building sites in the USA and Europe.

Chris's **Story**

Chris Gray says a roller-coaster experience is like a story.

THE BEGINNING

Chris begins by saying, "The beginning is where you see the massive roller-coaster at the amusement park. As you walk closer, it becomes larger, you hear its sounds and those of the people, too! You're feeling excited as you imagine yourself on that roller-coaster."

THE MIDDLE

"The story's middle is the actual roller-coaster ride and all its excitement," adds Chris.

> "A ROLLER-COASTER EXPERIENCE HAS A BEGINNING, A MIDDLE AND AN END."
>
> CHRIS GRAY

THE END

"For me, the end is when you leave the roller-coaster and walk away," says Chris.

Chris finishes by saying, "You have an amazing feeling and you have to talk about it with your family and your friends."

2 Roller-Coaster History

A **"Roller-Coaster"** on Ice!

an ice slide in Russia

Over 300 years ago, there were ice slides in Russia. They were the first rides that were like roller-coasters.

The person slid down the ice slide in a wooden or ice sled. Sand at the end of the slide, slowed the sled down until it stopped.

History and Social Studies

Great Coasters' History

Michael Boodley

The Great Coasters company is in Sunbury, Pennsylvania, USA. In 1996, Michael L. Boodley and Clair Hain started the company. They have built many roller-coasters with acrobatic track layouts that aim to deliver safe and thrilling rides for everyone to enjoy.

Science and Social Studies

Thomas Edison Wired in Sunbury

Thomas Edison

Thomas Edison was a famous inventor who was born in Ohio in 1847. In 1883, the city of Sunbury, Pennsylvania in the USA became famous when Edison wired one of the hotels so it could be the first to have electricity. Now it is called The Edison Hotel.

A Laundry Basket on Wheels

Michael Boodley is one of the founders of Great Coasters. He built his first roller-coaster as a boy. He put rollerskate wheels on the base of a laundry basket. The track was made from long wooden boards. His idea for wooden roller-coasters was born!

Michael in the laundry basket on wheels

Thrilling Twists and Turns

Today, Great Coasters is famous for designing and building wooden roller-coasters. Every roller-coaster has twists and turns so people have a ride that is thrilling but also safe!

Roller-Coaster Designs and Models

Who Wants a Roller-Coaster?

Amusement parks or theme parks order new roller-coasters. They want something that has never been seen before. A theme park in Florida, in the USA, asked Chris and his team at Great Coasters to design a new roller-coaster.

When Is the Roller-Coaster Named?

People at the amusement park named the roller-coaster, Gwazi. The name helped Chris and his team to think of many new ideas. It was exciting work for them!

Who Draws the Roller-Coaster?

After weeks of drawing in 2-D, Chris designed the Gwazi roller-coaster. It was going to be 1069 metres long, 32 metres high and roll at a speed of 82 kilometres per hour.

Chris worked out that the ride would run for about two minutes.

Chris designs at his desk

Why Build a Roller-Coaster Model?

Chris's next job was to use his 2-D drawings to build a 3-D model. He used balsa wood – the best wood for model-making. After it was built, the theme park and Great Coasters could see what the roller-coaster would look like. The model allows everyone to make changes before the real roller-coaster is built.

Design and Technology

Balsa Wood for Model-Making

Since the 1920s, many models have been built using balsa wood. Why do people use it? It is light, strong, easy to cut and bend into shape, and easy to glue together.

a roller-coaster model

the coolest photo Chris ever took

Roller-Coaster Building and Testing

Who **Builds** Roller-Coasters?

Chris and his team at Great Coasters take about 12 months to build a roller-coaster.

Roller-coasters are built over winter so they are ready to use in summer.

Who Tests Roller-Coasters?

Before people can ride a roller-coaster, it is tested for safety. Chris and his team check the parts carefully. This includes the brakes!

The first test is called a "roll over". It's when the roller-coaster trains are rolled over the tracks for the first time – without people on it.

Chris works in a snowstorm

checking under trains

When Is the First "Roll Over" a Success?

The "roll over" is a success when the trains reach the end safely. Chris Gray and his team smile, cheer and clap!

Health and Safety

Safety First

Chris's job involves many things but safety comes first. One example is the safety bar. A safety bar holds the riders in their seats. Chris goes to the factory where they are built to make sure that they are perfect.

Chris checks the safety bar

When Is the Best Time to Finish Building a Roller-Coaster?

Everyone wants their new roller-coasters ready just before summer. That's when most people go on holiday. Many go to amusement parks and theme parks. And what a surprise to see and ride on a great new roller-coaster!

Design and Technology

Roller-Coasters from Start to Finish

12 months

3 months

3 months

The first three months: design layout, build model, check the site and work out costing.

The next three months: write a contract between Great Coasters and the amusement park.

The next 12 months: build the roller-coaster.

5 Thunderbird Takes Flight

At **Powerpark** – West Finland

The Thunderbird is a wooden roller-coaster in the northernmost part of the world. It was built at Powerpark in Alahärmä in West Finland, Europe. The Thunderbird has a top speed of 75 kilometres per hour.

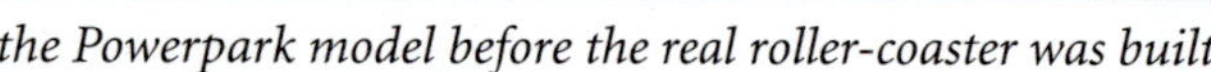

the Powerpark model before the real roller-coaster was built

the Thunderbird is finished

it's all downhill on the Thunderbird

6 How Do Roller-Coasters Work?

From **Station** to Station

1 THE STATION

This is where people get on and off the roller-coaster.

Feel the excitement as you put all safety equipment on!

2 LIFT HILL

The lift hill is where the roller-coaster train is "lifted" up to the top by chains.

Listen and you'll hear the clickety-click of the chains doing their job.

The roller-coaster has anti-rollback brakes, to make it safer.

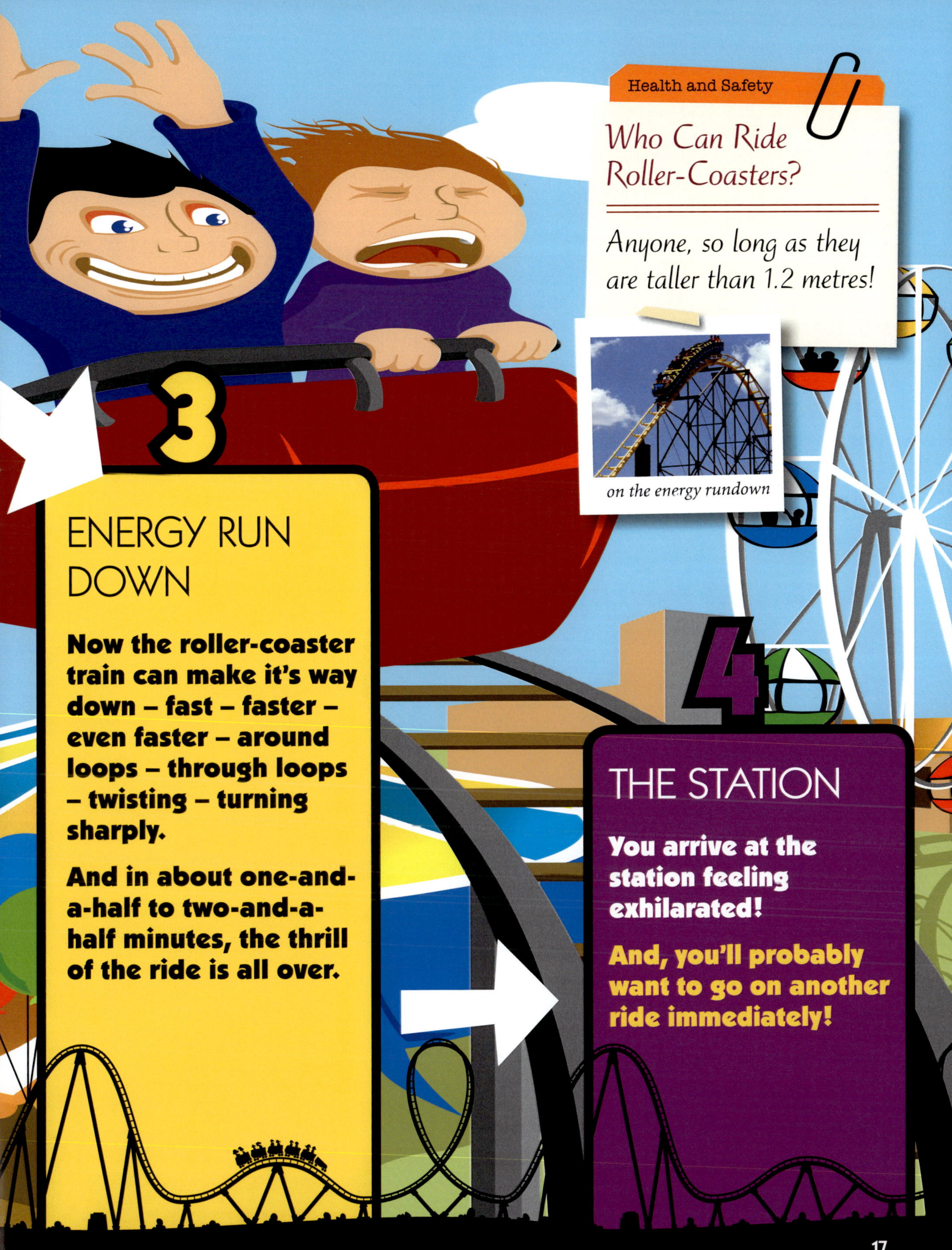

Health and Safety

Who Can Ride Roller-Coasters?

Anyone, so long as they are taller than 1.2 metres!

on the energy rundown

3

ENERGY RUN DOWN

Now the roller-coaster train can make it's way down – fast – faster – even faster – around loops – through loops – twisting – turning sharply.

And in about one-and-a-half to two-and-a-half minutes, the thrill of the ride is all over.

4

THE STATION

You arrive at the station feeling exhilarated!

And, you'll probably want to go on another ride immediately!

7 Amazing Roller-Coasters

Some **World-Famous** Roller-Coasters

The SMALLEST Roller-Coaster
Tusen Fryd – a 1.2 metre drop – Vinterbro, Norway

The LONGEST Steel Roller-Coaster
Steel Dragon – 2479 metres – Nagashima, Japan

The TALLEST Steel Roller-Coaster
Kingda Ka – 139 metres – Six Flags, New Jersey, USA

The OLDEST (working) wooden Roller-Coaster
Scenic Railway – 1912 – Melbourne, Australia

Physical Science

Speeding Down

The higher the lift hill, the more potential energy the roller-coaster train has. When it starts to go down, the energy becomes kinetic, or motion, energy. The more energy there is, the faster the roller-coaster ride!

The Scenic Railway goes down using kinetic energy.

The Great Coasters Chart

Ride	Height	Drop	Speed	Length
El Toro	24.5	21.5	73.4	725
Prowler	31.2	25.9	82.4	937
Terminator	29.0	26.6	80.6	877
Evel Knievel	25.0	24.4	77.2	827
Renegade 29.7	27.9	82.6	949	
Troy	31.9	30.7	86.9	1,077
Kentucky Rumbler	29.3	24.4	76.1	862
Thunderbird	25.0	24.4	77.2	827
Thunderhead	30.6	30.6	86.4	985
Ozark Wildcat	24.5	22.3	72.7	796
Lightning Racer	27.9	27.4	82.2	1,034
Gwazi	32.1	28.0	82.1	1,069
Roar (West)	28.8	25.9	81.3	1,057
Roar (East)	28.8	25.9	81.3	1,003
Wildcat	32.3	26.0	80.5	970

Height, drop and length are in metres and speed is kilometres per hour
Height measures the greatest difference of track elevation

the Prowler

the El Toro

the Steel Dragon in Japan

Elation!

8 Roller-Coaster Fun!

A **Summer** Holiday and More!

Q: What does Chris Gray do on holiday?

A: Well … ride roller-coasters of course!

Q: Why was the Liseberg roller-coaster Chris's favourite from the age of eight years?

the Liseberg, Sweden

A: It's not the fastest roller-coaster but he likes the way it is built on a hillside and uses the natural shape of the landscape.

Chris finally got to ride his favourite roller-coaster, the Liseberg.

In 2007, Chris rode 72 roller-coasters in 17 days! He rode them in six European countries – Germany, the Netherlands, Finland, Sweden, Norway and Denmark.

Finland

Norway

Sweden

Denmark

the Netherlands

Germany

TV Appearance

In 2008, a children's TV show in the USA, called *Design Squad* filmed a story about Chris and his work.

Roller-Coaster Awards

In 2005 and 2006, the Thunderbird roller-coaster won the award for the "Best Wooden Coaster in the World". This was a great honour for Chris Gray and his team!

Chris says, "It's called the Golden Ticket Awards – they're our version of the Academy Awards™!"

Trade Shows and Exhibitions

Companies can display their products and services at trade shows and exhibitions. Great Coasters attend trade shows all over the world to show customers what they make and do.

Customers are people from entertainment companies, such as amusement parks. When customers like the roller-coaster designs, they may ask Great Coasters to design a new roller-coaster for them, too.

Chris (centre, standing) at a trade show

Dolly's Roller-Coaster

Chris (centre back row) and his team enjoy a photo with Dolly Parton at Dollywood, USA. They built the Thunderhead roller-coaster for Dollywood in 2004.

The Prowler – A Landscape Roller-Coaster

In 2009, Chris and his team built the Prowler roller-coaster in Kansas, USA. It is set very low and it's fast! The roller-coaster is built around the natural landscape and it runs around the trees and drops over the hills.

Chris says, "Using the topography or the natural shape of the landscape is one of my favourite ways to design roller-coasters."

the Prowler

WHAT'S THE NEXT NEW Roller-COASTER?

Chris loves his work so much, he is always thinking of the next new roller-coaster idea.

He says, "I am always designing new and better roller-coasters.

I have built several models of roller-coasters at my home – it's still my passion."

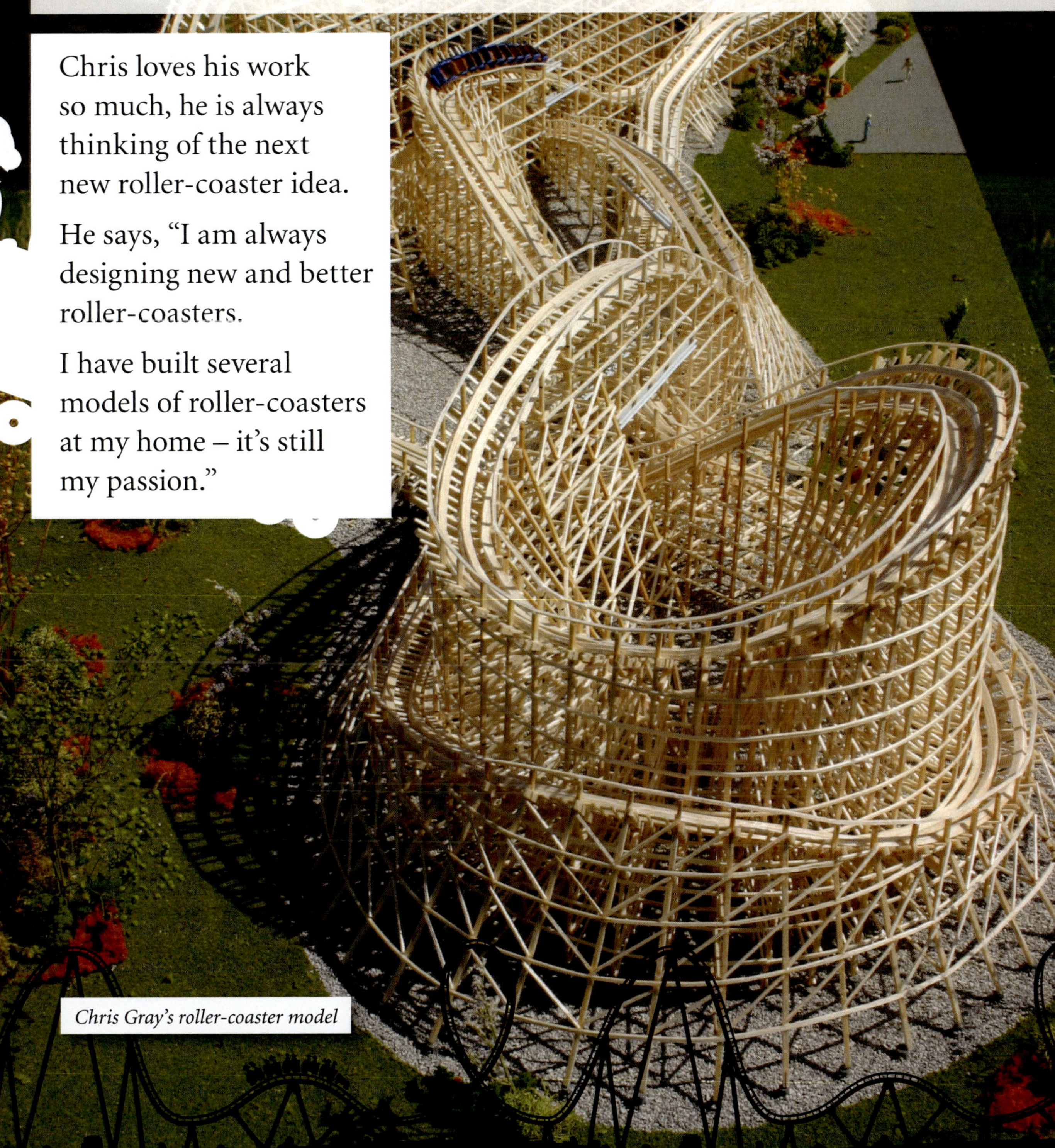

Chris Gray's roller-coaster model

Index

Glossary

anti-rollback brakes Brakes that are designed to stop a vehicle (such as a roller-coaster carriage) rolling backwards

contract A legal agreement between two or more people or groups to do something

costing Calculations that show how much people expect a thing or project will cost

engineer A person who designs how complicated systems (such as roller-coasters) will work

founders The people who first started a company or an organisation

potential energy The energy that an object stores up and that can be used or released later

procurement Buying of goods or services, usually for a large organisation

trade shows Meetings where people involved in the same industry display their goods and services